They Just, Don't get it!

Also by Leslie A. Yerkes

301 Ways to Have Fun at Work
(with Dave Hemsath)

Fun Works: Creating Places Where People Love to Work

Beans: Four Principles for Running a Business in Good Times or Bad
(with Charles Decker)

Business: The Ultimate Resource
(contributor)

Positively M.A. D. :
Making a Difference in Your Organizations, Communities, and the World
(contributor)

Also by Randy Martin

Are You Doing Business or Building One? :
Turning your business into your benefactor
(with Richard Zalack)

They Just Don't get it!

Changing resistance into understanding

BERRETT-KOEHLER PUBLISHERS, INC.
San Francisco

Berrett-Koehler Publishers, Inc.
235 Montgomery Street, Suite 650
San Francisco, CA 94104-2916
Tel: (415) 288-0260 Fax: (415) 362-2512 www.bkconnection.com

ORDERING INFORMATION
QUANTITY SALES. Special discounts are available on quantity purchases
by corporations, associations, and others. For details, contact the "Special
Sales Department" at the Berrett-Koehler address above.
INDIVIDUAL SALES. Berrett-Koehler publications are available through
most bookstores. They can also be ordered directly from Berrett-Koehler:
Tel: (800) 929-2929; Fax: (802) 864-7626; www.bkconnection.com
ORDERS FOR COLLEGE TEXTBOOK/COURSE ADOPTION USE. Please
contact Berrett-Koehler: Tel: (800) 929-2929; Fax: (802) 864-7626.
ORDERS BY U.S. TRADE BOOKSTORES AND WHOLESALERS. Please
contact Publishers Group West, 1700 Fourth Street, Berkeley, CA 94710.
Tel: (510) 528-1444; Fax: (510) 528-3444.
Berrett-Koehler and the BK logo are registered trademarks of Berrett-
Koehler Publishers, Inc.
PRINTED IN THE UNITED STATES OF AMERICA
Berrett-Koehler books are printed on long-lasting acid-free paper. When it is
available, we choose paper that has been manufactured by environmentally
responsible processes. These may include using trees grown in sustainable
forests, incorporating recycled paper, minimizing chlorine in bleaching, or
recycling the energy produced at the paper mill.

LIBRARY OF CONGRESS CATALOGING-IN-PUBLICATION DATA

Yerkes, Leslie, 1958-
    They just don't get it! : changing resistance into understanding / Leslie
Yerkes & Randy Martin.— 1st ed.
    p. cm.
    ISBN-13: 978-1-57675-328-6
1. Communication in management. 2. Influence (Psychology) 3. Per-
suasion (Psychology) I. Title.
    HD30.3.Y47 2005
    153.8'52—dc22

FIRST EDITION
10 09 08 07 06 05   10 9 8 7 6 5 4 3 2 1

Produced and designed by Randy Martin, martinDESIGN
Illustrations by Ben Dewey
Copy editing by Susan Martin; Linda DeVore, DeVore Associates.

To Jules Feiffer and Jimmy Buffett
whose expeditions into the unknown
showed the world they got it,
even if no one else did.
And to Walt Kelly whose Pogo once said
"We have met the enemy and he is us."

Contents

Preface

THEY JUST DON'T GET IT! is about those times when you're trying to tell someone something and they just don't get it, and what you need to do to transform their resistance into understanding.

If that sounds familiar, it should. Study after study shows us that the two most common problems in business are communication and resistance to change. In other words, *most* issues and problems in nearly *every* organization come down to the same thing: They just don't get it!

Typically, each of us looks at this situation as the other person's failing. We wonder—both silently and aloud—why they don't get it, why our brilliant explanations fall on apparently deaf ears. "I don't get it when they don't get it" is a song we sing, by ourselves and in a chorus with others. And each of us has been on the receiving end ourselves, having that song sung to us because we clearly weren't getting it.

In our role as change management consultants, we have observed thousands of leaders, managers, entrepreneurs, parents, and vested individuals dance the "I don't get it when they don't get it" tango. *They Just Don't Get It* puts this real-life situation up for discussion using the parable format, illustrated with fun, clever line drawings by Ben Dewey.

They Just Don't Get It gives owners, entrepreneurs, and managers insight into the reason their ideas don't get accomplished in the manner they expect; provides behavioral suggestions that help achieve goals in the future; and allows each of us to become aware of our personal responsibility in helping others understand our intentions.

Changing resistance into understanding is a conscious decision that is more about us than it is about them. When we focus only on them, we perpetuate the push-pull struggle. And so long as we are self-righteous, we will be met with resistance.

When it seems like they are not getting it, it is our responsibility to look at ourselves and our approach in a different light, suspend our judgment on their inability to understand, and look at the situation as an opportunity to grow, stretch, learn, and teach. Once we discover how best to engage them with the information, we need to believe passionately that they will be able to get it and succeed.

They Just Don't Get It is a story about changing from not getting it to really getting it. It's a unique opportunity to understand the root source of resistance and how, with enlightened awareness on our part, to overcome and prevent resistance in the future.

They Just Don't Get It provides the reader with personal insight into how to become a better communicator of ideas and an inspired motivator of people, both personally and professionally.

They Just Don't Get It helps each of us see that when they don't get it, the solution is really with us. As Pogo once said, "We have met the enemy and he is us."

So get comfortable, remove those distractions that might not let you focus on what you're reading, and get ready for a story that just might be more about you than it is about them.

Acknowledgments

GOOD STORIES ARE ABOUT PEOPLE; the best stories are about good people; great stories come from great people. Based on the people who have helped us put *They Just Don't Get It* together, this should be a great book. If it isn't, the fault lies with us, not with them.

These great folks include: our families and friends, our neighbors, our clients, our teammates, and our colleagues. You know who you are.

A special thanks goes to B.J. Gallagher, whose many business fable books, notably *A Peacock in the Land of Penguins*, have shown us the way.

Thanks always go to Steve Piersanti, Publisher in Chief, Berrett-Koehler Publishing, for his faith, trust, and insight. And to the Berrett-Koehler team who have pushed us to make this book what it is. Their devotion to creating books of quality is what make Berrett-Koehler a leader in the publishing industry.

The fact that they got it about *They Just Don't Get It*, speaks to their abilities as publishers of books that teach individuals how to be better at business, life, and getting it.

We hope *They Just Don't Get It* helps you get it; but more than that we hope it helps you help *them* to get it.

Leslie Yerkes, Randy Martin
Cleveland, Ohio
March 2005

They Just, Don't get it!

Part
One
Pulling
Apart

Chapter One 1

There once was a woman named Julie who lived in the very best apartment atop the very best building in the very best city in America.

Julie's apartment was filled with the very best things she could buy.

She owned a top-of-the-line high definition television set with theater surround sound, a treadmill with automatic memory and thirty-five presets of the most famous terrain in the world, and a chrome espresso machine that her father said reminded him of the '58 Buick he used to own.

Julie had the very best job anyone could imagine. She was the senior vice president and chief account executive for the very best advertising agency in town.

She had the very best clients and produced the very best advertising in America.

Everything that Julie did was superb; everything she owned was better; every idea she had was the very best. In short, Julie got it.

All her friends said so. They said things to each other like, "You know why Julie does so well? It's simple. Julie gets it."

Which is why this morning was so troubling to Julie.

Julie wasn't interested in watching television. She wasn't interested in making espresso.

And she certainly wasn't interested in running up the side of Mount Kilimanjaro, although she could have.

And she wasn't interested in doing all these very best things because her head hurt.

Julie's head had hurt since she woke up two hours before. Before her alarm even went off.

Julie woke with a headache caused by a question that had been bouncing around in her brain all night long while she tried to sleep.

She had this awful, annoying question because for the first time in her life, Julie had come face-to-face with something she didn't get.

It was a simple question. One that all of us ask, all the time, of far too many people, far too often.

It's a question that causes us to lose sleep. And to not understand. And to not finish projects. And to lose friends.

And, although it really is a simple question to ask, it's one of the most difficult ones in the world to answer.

So what is this simple but profound question? The question that was bouncing around in Julie's head?

Here it is.

This is it.

This is the question:

Why don't they get it?

Chapter Two 2

Julie's head hurt. It hurt so bad that she did something she had never done before in her life: She called in sick and climbed back into bed.

When did this pain first begin? she wondered, as she rolled her pillow into a ball and pulled her very best linen comforter over her head. *Was it last night, or did it start sometime even sooner?*

Maybe my journal will have the answer! she thought. She reached over to the nightstand, pulled the journal to her, and started to read what she'd written the last several days.

And there was her answer . . . in her own handwriting.

Of course! It *was* yesterday! During The Doodley Sauerkraut Company presentation.

She had just gone through all the elements of the new campaign and was finishing up with the TV spot about the alligator eating a Reuben sandwich without the Russian dressing when Doodley's president, J. Worthington Swag, said, "I just don't get it, Julie. I thought this was supposed to be funny!"

"What do you mean, you don't get it?" she had said, shocked not only at the question but that anyone wouldn't understand the obvious symbolism.

"The alligator loves your sauerkraut so much he doesn't want to spoil it with the dressing! It's hysterical!"

"But why an alligator?"

"Because alligators are funny!" she'd told him, her voice climbing a few pitches toward high C.

"Look at Wally Gator! A laugh-a-minute!"

"I didn't care for him either," JW replied without even a smile.

" I just don't get what's funny about alligators. Do alligators eat corned beef?"

"Who cares?"

"Can they hold a sandwich in their claws? And even if they could hold it, could they reach their mouth with it? I just don't get it!"

That's where it had started, all right.

With J. Worthington Swag.

What was wrong with clients like him? Why didn't they get it?

The alligator gambit was so obvious, and hilariously funny.

Why was old JW so clueless?

Though, to be honest, it wasn't just JW who didn't get it. John, her assistant, wasn't sure alligators were funny either.

Now that she thought about it, she hadn't really been able to get John on board from the beginning. Nothing she had told him seemed to convince him or even make him understand.

Maybe she needed to rethink John's role in the creative group.

And Mary Sue, too!

As the head writer on the campaign, Mary Sue wanted to make the lead character a koala bear, for heaven's sake!

Talk about not getting it!

Koala bears aren't funny! They're cuddly!

They only eat eucalyptus leaves and *no one* puts sauerkraut on eucalyptus leaves!

What was wrong with these people, Julie thought. Why don't they get it?

I DON'T GET IT WHEN THEY DON'T GET IT!

Julie was having a hard time with this simple question. All this thinking was making her head hurt.

She was confused, and it was all *their* fault!

So she did what she always did in tough times like this.

She rolled over and went back to sleep.

Chapter Three 3

Not getting it was taking its toll on Julie.

She slept the rest of the day.

When she finally awoke, it was just around midnight. Julie was hungry and her head still hurt.

And still, she didn't get it.

Not that it mattered if *she* didn't get it. It wasn't her problem; it was theirs. They were the ones who really didn't get it. They were the problem.

My problem, she thought, *is that I'm hungry.*

So she got up and went into the kitchen to find something to eat. But all she had in her pantry was a case of Doodley's Sauerkraut.

And she certainly wasn't that hungry.

So she ordered Chinese.

While she waited for her dinner to arrive, she went online to see what she could research about people not getting it.

She was surprised at what she found.

It seems that people have been not getting it for some time.

Ancient people didn't think it was possible to create fire. They thought that fire existed only as a gift from the gods.

The King of Portugal didn't get it when
Columbus wanted to sail around the world on
the king's dime.

The King and Queen of Spain kind of got it.
But they were more interested in finding
treasure than in knowing whether or not the
world was round.

Nobody got it when Galileo claimed the earth revolved around the sun.

Although, Galileo got it later for trying to make everyone else get what he got.

And nobody got it when Thomas Edison said he could make a light bulb or record the human voice singing a song.

Until he made it happen.

Then we *all* got it.

The list of people who didn't get it, like the result of so many online searches, went on and on and on.

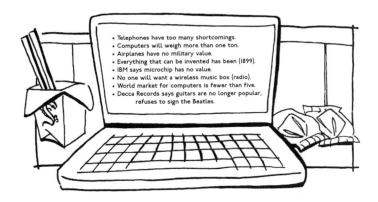

- Telephones have too many shortcomings.
- Computers will weigh more than one ton.
- Airplanes have no military value.
- Everything that can be invented has been (1899).
- IBM says microchip has no value.
- No one will want a wireless music box (radio).
- World market for computers is fewer than five.
- Decca Records says guitars are no longer popular, refuses to sign the Beatles.

While Julie ate her Kung Pao Chicken, she thought about how Mom and Dad didn't get it when she was a teenager, and she wanted to drive her friends to the beach for the day, and they wouldn't let her—but she did it anyway.

Or how they didn't get it that she wanted to have a career in advertising instead of working in the family bookstore back in Wooster.

She wondered if they got it now that she was successful in her chosen field.

But if they didn't, too bad.

It always was *their* problem.

She was certain that if she were going to get some guidance in figuring out this pain in her head, it wasn't going to come from Mom or Dad.

And it certainly wasn't going to fall from the sky like a gift from the gods.

Maybe she'd better make an appointment with Professor Rudolph for tomorrow.

Part Two

Gaining Understanding

Chapter Four 4

"It's something that happens as we mature, Julie. The older we get, the more fallible we become. We know less compared to how much there is to know, but more about what's important and what we *need* to know.

"How you learn to deal with this reality determines how well *you* get the things that go on all around you all the time."

What does that mean? she wondered as she walked down the cold and windy canyon-like streets of the best city in America. *I thought you were supposed to get smarter and better the older you got.*

What Dr. R said sounded like just the opposite.

Now I really don't get it—even more.

Or is that less?

I guess if I got it, I'd know.

But I don't.

Why is it that some people get it right away? she wondered. *Like Joel, her artist, got the Doodley campaign thing. He even understood the alligator concept. But no amount of telling John and Mary Sue the same concepts over and over seemed to make a dent.*

Some folks get it, some folks never seem to.

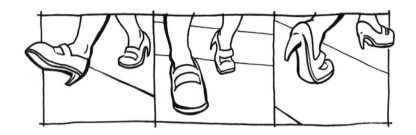

Julie walked and thought.

She thought she needed to find out what was going on. And information, she felt, was the key to discovering why some people got it and some people simply didn't.

One thing she thought as she continued walking was that she'd have to write all this down in her journal once she got home.

But where was she now? She had been so focused on the inside of her head that she had no clue what was going on outside all around her.

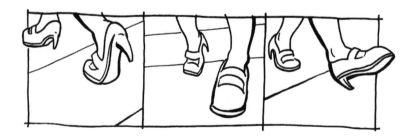

When she looked, she discovered she had
walked all the way to the sea.

Or at least to the boardwalk that goes along
the shoreline of one of the greatest lakes in the
world.

And right past the door of a fortune teller,
Madame Nosall, The Cajun Seer.

"How did you know my name and what I wanted?"

"Do you think Madame Nosall knows nothing? Now, sit you down and 'fess up. What is this thing you don't get, child?"

"I don't get it when *they* don't get it. It seems so obvious to me. Yet, when I try to explain it, they act like they don't even hear me—much less understand me."

"Do you know what I mean?"

Julie waved her hands in exasperation and slumped in her chair.

"Honey, I know more than that. *Everyone* I deal with don' get it. That's why they come to me."

"But when they leave here, do they get it? Or are they upset with themselves that you had to tell them what they didn't know when they walked in here in the first place?"

"They ain' upset at all, no. They may not believe me, but they don't be dissettled none. An' you know why? I tell you why, you.
"See, when they come to me they already tol' themselves they don't know.
"So they willin' to listen."

"Why doesn't that work for me?" Julie asked, sighing audibly.

"Cuz when *you* see they don't get it, *you* don't listen to them, no, *you* start talking a li'l louder, a li'l faster.
"And pretty soon you make it clear that *you* tink they not too smart, them. That *you* think they either stupid—or dumb.

"And when they think you think they dumb? Well . . . that make them not wanna listen no more, and they get furder and furder away from getting it theyselves."

"Oh, honey, you don' gotta say it wit' you mouth. You body got attitude, and you attitude say all they need a know, them.

"All they need a know, for sure."

"I really act like that?"

"Don't know why not. Everybody else seem to."

"But why, if I can see the answer so clearly, why can't they see it like I do? Why don't they get it, too?"

"Honey, it's like Desi say to Lucy,

Chapter Five 5

*Before I talked to Madame Nosall, I was
certain that it was all their fault that they
didn't get it,* Julie thought on her way home.

Now that she had been to see the gypsy and
had her fortune read, she wondered if maybe it
wasn't their fault after all. It just might be both
their faults.

And maybe them not getting it was
connected to her not explaining it very well.
Maybe she needed to listen more to them and
explain it their way and not hers.

Maybe them not getting it was a result of
the way she was giving it.

And if all this were true, she thought,
maybe I'm the one who has to make changes!

Just like the way my parents tried to tell me how to live my life made me rebel even more, Julie recalled.

That was true, wasn't it?

My rebellious teenage years were their fault and not mine—weren't they?

I mean, they wanted me to be Miss Goody Two Shoes, after all. I tried to tell them that simply wasn't me. But I don't think they ever understood that, she mused, walking back into the city deep in thought.

I simply don't know any more, Julie thought. *Maybe I'd better go and ask Mom and Dad right to their face. Yeah, that's it. I'll ask them what's going on. Maybe they can help me now that I'm a little older.*

It couldn't hurt to try, she thought.

And she raised her arm and began yelling at the top of her lungs:

Chapter Six 6

"Julie, dear. Do you remember those Chinese handcuffs your Aunt Lulu brought back from Singapore that time?"

"Yes, Mother, I do. Why are you asking me that now?

"I'm trying to find out why nobody in the world gets it but me, and you're asking me about souvenirs that Aunt Lulu gave me years ago."

"Dear, this *is* about your question. Do you remember how they worked?"

"How what worked, Mother?" Julie said distractedly, and with a fairly healthy touch of annoyance in her voice.

Just like always, she thought, *Mother's not only on another page, she's in another book.*

"The Chinese handcuffs, dear. Really. Stop thinking about yourself and try to remember when you were eight years old and Aunt Lulu put your pointer fingers in them.

"How hard did you have to pull before they came off? Do you remember?"

"Of course I remember, Mother.

"At first, I pulled hard and I couldn't make them budge. So I pulled even harder and still nothing happened.

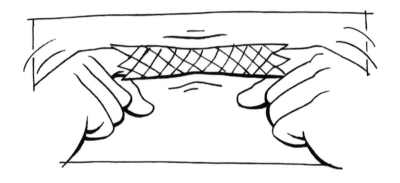

"Eventually, I got so tired that I just relaxed and moved my fingers slowly, and the handcuffs also relaxed and stopped fighting me, and then they came off!"

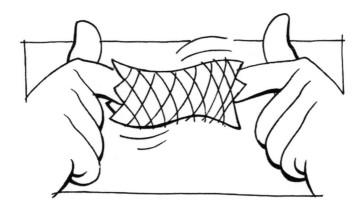

"That's right, dear. But strictly speaking, the handcuffs couldn't fight you because they weren't alive. They were only resisting your effort. They were designed so that the harder you pulled against them, the more resistance they generated.

"It's the same with the people around you. If you pull them or push them too hard, they will resist you and any effort you make to change them. If you ease up and give them time, and make an effort to include them in what's going on, they'll eventually come around to your point of view. Or at least they'll begin to listen to it. We all need consideration. Nobody likes to have their feelings or their ideas trampled on.

"And it's the same with you."

Julie was near tears. And, like a little girl in Chinese handcuffs, she was too tired to continue fighting, so she relaxed.

That's when her mother's message finally started to get through.

"Are you telling me that people around me don't get it because I push them too hard? That I don't listen? That I haven't explained it well enough for them to get it?

"Why didn't you tell me all this before, Mom? Dad?
"Why did I have go through my entire life making a fool of myself?"

"Getting it isn't an easy thing," her mother said. "We thought it was our duty while you were growing up to tell you how to do everything in your life, so that's what we did. The truth was, though, that even while we were telling you, we were learning. Getting it is something that takes all your life. It's like Ethel Barrymore said, 'It's what you learn after you know it all that counts.'"

"Ethel Barrymore was an actress a long time ago," her dad said, even before Julie could say a word. Then he asked her to sit down and tell him some more of what she'd learned from Madame Nosall.

Julie and her parents talked for hours, sharing their stories about getting it. Slowly, Julie began to realize that everyone in the world was having the same problem getting it as she was.

I think that's what they mean by "Misery loves company," Julie thought. *We're all in the same boat together.*

Later that evening, after reflecting all the way home on what she'd heard and learned, Julie collected her thoughts in her journal.

Chapter Seven 7

Wednesday, July 12

This has been a very difficult few days. Learning lots of things about why THEY just don't get it.

Mostly, though, I think I've learned that when they don't get it, that doesn't mean it's their fault. I've got a lot to do with how well they get what I mean.

Here's a summary of what I've discovered the last few days.

(Note: Make a copy of this and put it somewhere at work where I can check it when I need to.)

* When they don't get it, it's less about them and more about me. And what I'm doing or not doing.

* Change is not the same for everybody. For some of us it's easier than for others.

* Some people understand your vision immediately; some take longer. Some never get it. And that's no one's fault. It just is.

* Everyone needs their questions answered and their fears addressed or they will move away from getting it.

* Everyone needs consideration. We are all people with feelings and ideas.

* If pushed or pulled, people will fight to remain rooted. If coaxed with knowledge and invited to participate, they will learn to move on their own toward the common goal.
(Remember Aunt Lulu's handcuffs!)

* When I apply all of the above, people transform. When they transform, they get it. When they get it, they are confident they can do it.

* Finally, I've learned that when they don't get it, it's not necessarily a bad thing.

Because when they don't get it, that's my opportunity to become a teacher and a partner and to see to it that we all get it together!

Tomorrow I'm going to get the chance to try out what I've learned.

I'm looking forward to it.

Part
Three

Pulling
Together

Chapter Eight 8

"I've heard you talk a lot about this alligator and the sauerkraut," John said, a little edge in his voice, "but I have to say, I still don't get it. I guess I'm with Doodley on this one. I don't think an alligator is funny at all."

This was exactly where they were two days ago, Julie thought. *Only last time, I pushed John and Mary Sue so hard that all they did was stop talking; that made me think I'd convinced them.*

When we got to the presentation, she recalled, *it was clear that I was on my own.*

This time is going to be different, she vowed.

"Joel," Julie said, catching John and Mary Sue off guard, "You seem to understand what I'm going for here. You want to tell us why? What's your take on all this?"

Now this was certainly different, Mary Sue thought while she listened to Joel. *Creative meetings before were never much more than Julie telling us what she wanted us to do. Lucky for us she was almost always right.*

But this is something different. Something new.

Maybe I'd better listen real good.

"Well, Julie," Joel said, a little surprised to be asked to express his opinion, but pleased nonetheless, "to be honest, I wasn't all that convinced the main character *should* have been an alligator. But I knew exactly what the joke was."

"If you didn't think it should have been an alligator, what did you do to make it work in your head?" Julie asked.

"Well," Joel said, as he smiled, "I just thought of a gorilla, you know? Like Sampson in the Milwaukee zoo? And gorillas are so much more human-like. So whenever I thought about the alligator, I just pictured Sampson. You know, when he was putting the sauerkraut on his sandwich?"

As Joel got into his story, Julie could see that Mary Sue and John were connecting with what he was saying, and they were making suggestions, too!

Maybe this getting it wasn't so difficult after all, once you realized that getting it wasn't simply their problem, Julie thought.

This is working far better than I could have hoped for. I can't wait to call J. Worthington Swag and schedule a new meeting date for our new presentation.

This was going to be great!

The best campaign ever!

Chapter Nine 9

"Mr. Swag? Julie Buffet here. I wonder if we could come over to your office sometime tomorrow. We've been going over the questions you had on the campaign and we think you're right about the alligator.

"We've made some changes and we'd like to show them to you personally . . .

'For lunch? Sure . . . Oh, of course! We all love Reubens.

"See you later.

"And thanks, Mr. Swag.

"Bye!"

Chapter Ten 10

The presentation today was terrific. Joel's idea to change the lead from the alligator (which was kind of dumb, now that I think about it) to a gorilla was brilliant. I don't think I've ever seen or heard Mr. Swag laugh so much in my life.

And John and Mary Sue did a terrific job of tag-teaming the presentation. Their role playing is some of the best I've ever seen. I didn't know they had it in them.

It's hard to believe we were able to turn the presentation around like that. Actually, it isn't hard to believe my team members did it. I always knew they could. It's really more about me and the way I'm changing how I go about getting it. Professor Rudolph, Mom and Dad, and Madame Nosall were so much help. I don't know where I'd be without them. I'm glad I stopped trying so hard to be right and decided to listen to what they had to say. It sure made a difference.

Tomorrow should be interesting. I plan to bring up this "get it" concept with the creative team and see if they have any insight. My old approach would have been simply to tell them what I've learned and try to make them understand. I'll be interested to see if I've actually learned anything at all.

Chapter Eleven 11

"We did it! We hit it out of the park, knocked Swag dead!" Mary Sue said as she hugged Julie.

Julie and her creative team were in the corporate conference room celebrating their successful presentation of the revised Doodley Sauerkraut campaign. Unlike the first one, this presentation had been a real team effort, and they were all very proud of their work.

"I'm so proud of you all," Julie beamed.

"What a great presentation," John agreed.

"Too bad we didn't start out like this," Joel said.

Every member of the team stopped short at Joel's insight, then nodded their head in agreement.

"I have to admit," said Julie, "I was just a little bit frustrated with all of you back when I was trying to explain my original concept. I just couldn't believe you didn't get it."

"I think we all felt the same way about you," Mary Sue said. "You spent all your time explaining things to us but you didn't seem to spend *any* time listening."
The others nodded their agreement again.

"So what we're saying," Julie said, trying to find a common kernel of truth in their comments, "is that when I think *you* don't get it . . . you think *I* don't get it. Is that it?"

"I think you've got it!" Joel laughed.

"For me," Joel continued, "when the whole group isn't on the same page, I get frustrated. And either I find myself disconnecting from you all or I seem to get stuck where I am and then I give up and give in."

"And what we get," Julie added, "is work that isn't our best."

For a few moments, everyone stopped talking and went deep into thought.

Then Julie asked, "Do you think this happens to us a lot?"

"It doesn't happen all the time," Joel said. "If it did we wouldn't be the very best agency in town, but it does happen. Remember Kingly Nut?"

Everyone shuddered as they recalled that terrible project. When Kingly pulled their account—because they didn't like the new campaign—Julie actually considered breaking up her creative group. And they considered leaving to join another team.

Not a bright day in any of their lives.

"You're right, Joel. That was awful. During that project our energy and creativity were the lowest I can ever remember, and our frustration was the highest," Julie recalled.

John added, "The result we got wasn't anything close to the amount of effort we put in. It seemed like the harder we worked to convince each other that our way was the right way, the further away we got from understanding each other. We were pulling apart instead of pulling together."

"Wow! That's powerful, John," Joel said with admiration.

"What happened, if you remember," Julie continued, "was that after we pulled apart, we had a meltdown and started sniping at each other. Then, we just sort of agreed to accept what we had, rather than continue the creative process."

"Lucky for us that doesn't happen all the time," Mary Sue said.

"Yeah," Julie added. "When we're on, we get along well, the ideas flow, and we have a good time. When we get it, it doesn't even seem like work."

"It's too bad we can't figure out how to make sure we get it all the time," John said.

"Maybe we could if we were fancy management consultants, but I don't know the right words," Mary Sue said. "Do you?"

"Sure!" Julie said excitedly. "It's not about knowing *their* words, it's about finding *our* words so that what we say makes sense to us. It doesn't do anyone any good to simply parrot back what *they* say. If you really understand something — if you really get it — then you can explain it using *your* words!

"I know! Why don't we just do what we do: think about this as if it were a problem presented to us by a client — one that they wanted us to solve for them?"

"Yeah!" Joel said, clearly in the midst of getting it. "What we need to do is to create the 'Get It!' campaign."

They all agreed and so they did.

For the next several hours, Julie, Joel, John, and Mary Sue brain stormed.

They mind mapped.

They dialogued.

They talked and they listened—to each other and to John play Jimmy Buffett over and over and over again on his boom box.

And they had fun.

Instead of trying to convince each other of their *own* point of view, they each tried to discover what the other person meant by the words they were using.

And when they did, they put it all down on paper. Using the words they all knew, in the way they understood the best.

Chapter Twelve 12

"Joel, why don't you do the honors?" Julie suggested. "You do the presentation and we'll be the client. Okay?"

"Well, I don't know. I'm just an artist."

"Come on, Joel," Mary Sue said. "Without your gorilla, we'd never be here in the first place. You can do it! Go for it!"

Joel did just that, and this is what he said:

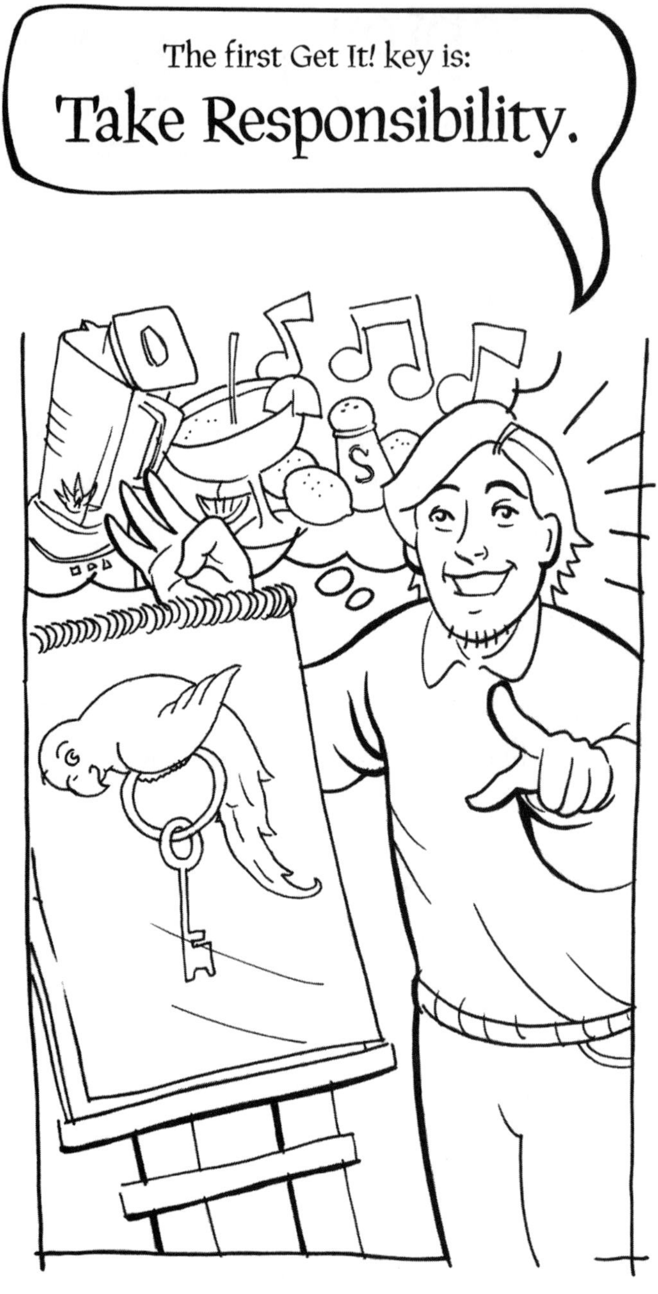
The first Get It! key is:
Take Responsibility.

"This might be the most difficult key because until we accept it, we don't stand a chance of getting it. Programmed into all of us, it seems, is this desire to find out why something didn't work and whose fault it was. We all want to know who to blame for our problems. And yet, most of our parents reminded us as we grew up that we're supposed to take responsibility for what we do.

"However, *my* inspiration for this key comes from the Jimmy Buffet song that John loves to play over and over on our CD player: *Margaritaville*. As I'm sure you recall, the singer starts by saying that the problem he and his girl friend are having is all her fault. And as the song goes on, he starts to consider that the problem might be both their faults, until he ends by saying the problem is his own damn fault.

"That's the lesson here: The problem is less about them than it is about us. And once we get that, we get it. And we stop fixing blame and start finding a solution.

"Don't Place Blame; Take Responsibility."

"The inspiration for this one was the story Julie told us about her Aunt Lulu and the Chinese handcuffs," Joel said, as he warmed to his role as presenter. "You remember how the more you pulled, the harder the handcuffs stuck to your fingers? That's the example that started us off. But I think it was Mary Sue's story about the workshop she attended that got us to see how this key applies to all of us in everyday situations. You were asked to pick a partner. You made a fist and your partner had ten seconds to get your hand open. Most people tried some type of force, pulling the fingers open one at a time, even tickling.

"But the more force they applied, the harder the person clenched their fist. Then Mary Sue had a bright idea: She simply asked her partner to open her fist, and she did.

"Force is our natural reaction to solving problems. Often, however, force produces the least effective results. When we relax, remain confident, and learn to encourage full participation and not use force, we achieve our intentions. It's what we call being humble, admitting you don't know everything and asking for help rather than trying to make them be just like you.

"Force Begets Resistance; Practice Humility."

The third Get It! key is:
Begin with Questions.
are you in
DO YOU LOVE

"This key comes directly from Advertising Copy Writing 101. As you know, when you really want someone to buy something, the last thing you do is tell them that. Most good copy, and all the great direct mail advertising copy, begins with a question: 'Are you the kind of person who . . . ?' or 'Does this sound like you?' or 'What would you do with a million dollars?'

"When we try to tell people what to do, their first reaction is to hold back. When Julie started asking us questions about alligators and sauerkraut was when we started coming up with answers. Soon, we had all sorts of ideas, far more than we could actually use. In life, just as in advertising, the fatal trap is to try to *sell* them when you could be asking questions that *engage* them.

"Telling Turns Them Off; Use the Power of Questions."

"This key comes from Madame Nosall telling Julie to begin by not trying to be right. It's reminiscent of a tug-of-war: both sides pulling with all their might in order to win, to get the other people on their side. While this is fun to do at picnics, a tug-of-war over ideas always results in someone falling down, getting hurt and dirty, at least figuratively. The winning side feels powerful, dominant; the losing side weak, dominated. The balance of power in that situation is off, and so is the way both sides feel about each other. In a tug-of-war, there is no win-win, only win-lose.

"Sometimes in a tug-of-war, when the outcome appears hopeless, one side might simply give up and let go. When that happens, the other side falls to the ground. Winning may have been their goal, but the way in which it happened was not satisfying and they feel awkward. For us, that means our clients probably don't get our best work.

"If we're open to ideas, and we don't try to pull people over to our side, then we're able to share our ideas, listen to their ideas, and then pick and choose which parts of both sides could be combined to make the best final result.

"Being Right Might Be Wrong; Remain Open."

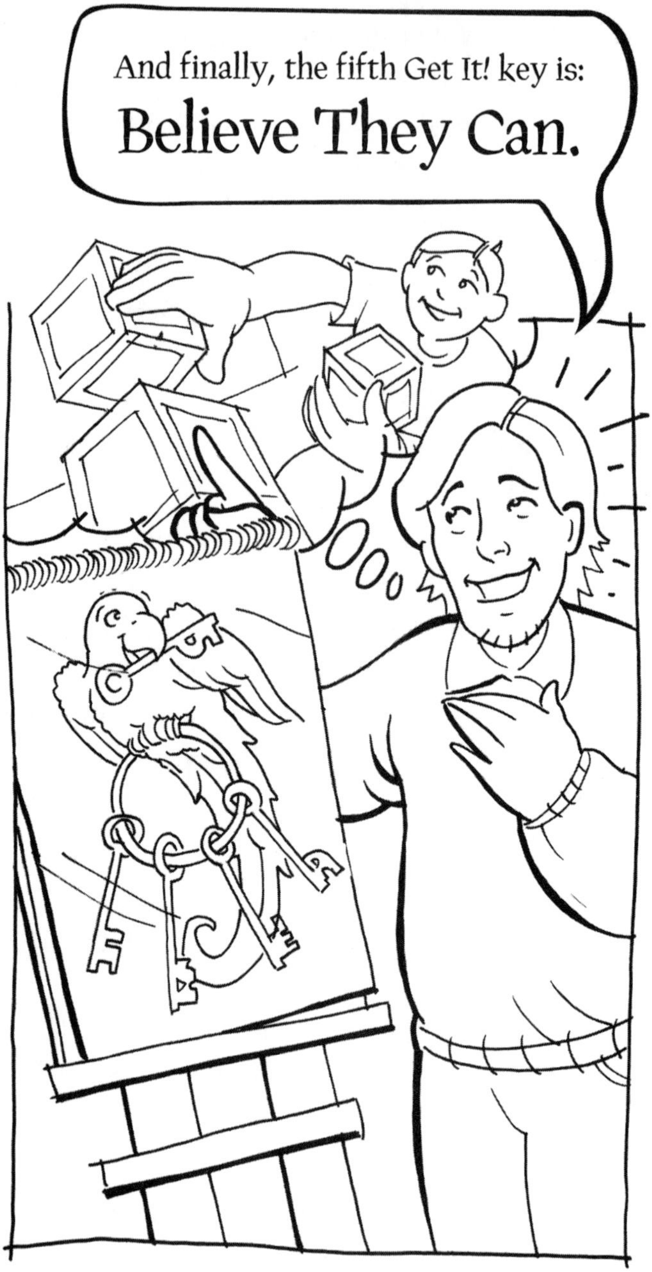
And finally, the fifth Get It! key is:
Believe They Can.

"We have that poster on the wall with Henry Ford's quote: 'Whether you think you can or you think you can't, you're right.'

"And that talks about how each one of us needs to think about ourselves and our abilities in order to succeed. But there's a story I like to tell about my son that tells me how I have to think about other people.

"One day Matthew was busy putting together some blocks on the floor. I asked him what he was doing, and he told me what he was making. Being the wise grown-up, I told him, 'That will never work.' He looked up at me and without missing a beat said, 'I have to think it will.'

"And that's the message: We have to think it will. If Julie didn't think we could get it, she wouldn't have tried a second time with the Doodley campaign. She would have written off both it and us. We all need to expect success if we want success to happen.

"If You Believe They Can't, They Won't; Believe They Can."

"So there you have it, ladies and gentlemen, the Get It! campaign, courtesy of the very best advertising agency in the city: us!

"I thank you for your time.

"And I hope you all Get It!"

"Wow!"

"That was great, Joel!"

"Yeah, great! Terrific!"

The moment Joel had finished his presentation, the whole team jumped up and began to shake hands and high-five each other. They talked so fast it was hard to tell who was saying what. But they all agreed: They were starting to get it.

And it was fun.

Finally, Julie said to the group, "This is wonderful. Now each of us knows how to make sure we get it, every time. And if we just keep Joel's presentation in mind, we can get it every time we have a new project."

"Yeah, and every time we make a presentation," Joel said. "And that, by the way, that was my *last* presentation. *Ever!*"

They all laughed and then Mary Sue said, "We have to make sure that not only do we know how to get it, but that our clients know how to get it, too."

"Why stop there?" said John, who liked to think big. "Why not tell the whole world?
"Let's put this in a book so that everyone will be able to Get It!"

And so they did.

The End

Part
Four

Learning
to Understand

Learning
to
Understand

HOW MANY TIMES HAVE YOU FOUND yourself say-ing that you just don't get it when they don't get it? Or asking yourself why it is that you see the solution so clearly when they don't have a clue? Why, when the need to change is so obvious even a child would get it, do they remain ignorant?

When we find ourselves in the position of being amazed that *they* don't get it, we automatically spring to action and assume the role of Chief Getting It Instruc-tor. Our voice takes on a particular tone, our face assumes a parental mask, and our body portrays a superior pos-ture. And we step into our self-appointed role of guiding the unenlightened into the light, the light of getting it.

Surprisingly, those tutorial garments of attitude, in-flection, and posture cause the folks we are trying to help to turn off, turn away. We discourage their participation, and close down their channels of understanding.

What do we do then? Do we become more insistent? More cynical? Do we find ourselves saying "How many times am I going to have to tell you before you under-stand?" If they still don't get it, or even seem to try to get it, do we withhold our support? Do we give up, deter-mining them to be ignorant and unreachable?

Do we complain about them to others? Raise our voice, yell, tell, preach? Our voice gathering steam while their eyes glaze over?

And don't we find that the more we try to get through to them, the more right we become? Maybe even self-righteous?

THE MORE ENERGY WE EXPEND trying to change people, the more we seem to stimulate the opposite result from the one we intended to achieve; not only don't they get it, but they seem to take two steps backwards! And though our intentions may be good, they give no sign of appreciating our intentions, our efforts, or even us. Our gesture (our attempt at doing a good deed) is misunderstood, and it creates all sorts of new issues to unravel.

That's when we want to throttle them. Or just let the looming negative consequences of not getting it fall on their thick heads. At which point we could feel righteous because, after all, we tried to tell them. And we could rest easy knowing we were right.

Unfortunately, although we might be right, they still don't get it and whatever problem we originally faced remains. Only now things are even worse.

SO, WHAT DO YOU DO WHEN they don't get it? When they do not or will not participate? Is it your job to make sure they do? To change them so that they do get it? Could you change them even if you wanted to? If they don't change, what is the consequence to you or to them?

And could that be the key to all this? That not getting it is really about you as much as it is about them?

If it is about us, then it's we who need to make the

changes. All of us need to change, adapt, and move forward. The problem is that none of us change in the same way, at the same time, or at the same rate. There are those of us who can envision change and begin to move toward it with ease. These agents of change challenge our attachment to the way we are doing things. Sometimes the challenges are tactful and diplomatic; sometimes forceful and passionate—like a force of nature.

Some of us may not get it at first, but when our questions are answered and our fears addressed, we get it with relative ease. Our craving is information; our need is consideration. When these are met, we respond, we participate. When we are pushed or pulled, we remain rooted in "the way we've always done it," in what we know how to do. To get it, we need help understanding that which we do not know.

And, of course, there are always some of us who choose not to get it. Staying put is our choice. We will filibuster in favor of not getting it. To us, not getting it becomes a virtue, a banner under which to lead an army of recalcitrants. And we become the rock on which people use their biggest "I just don't get it when they don't get it" hammer.

SO, IS THERE A PERFECT RESPONSE to the trap of "I don't get it when they don't get it?" Is there a solution? If you are given a prescription to deal with their not getting it, will that make it better? Or have we only scratched the surface of an iceberg? What happens if you don't like my solution? Or understand it? Or you reject it? Or you use it differently than I intended, creating different results that you blame me for causing?

What if all those questions lead to yet another one, one that might finally give us a solution? What if we ask ourselves this question:

What could I do or say that would help them understand what they need to know to succeed? To get it?

Or this question:
What kind of environment would support them in finding the information they need to realize their own change?

Or these:
How can I model behaviors that will illustrate the desired state? How can I create opportunities for them to participate and try on new styles or behaviors without feeling endangered?

What stands in the way of their getting it? Is it as simple as: "This is the way we've always done it"? If so, how do we respectfully challenge that comfort zone? What questions can we ask, not as interrogator but as supportive friend, that would promote their own process of reflection and exploration?

THERE ARE SEVERAL KEYS TO DEALING with the "I don't get it when they don't get it" syndrome, which, if applied, will help us unlock the secrets of getting it, of moving toward things under own motivation—without resistance.

Get It!
Key One
Don't Place Blame;
Take Responsibility

HENRY FORD SAID, "Don't fix the blame, fix the problem: Find a solution." In the ultimate scheme of things, who did what to whom is not beneficial information nor is it required to improve the situation. And if improving the situation is your goal, why spend time and effort on fixing blame? Or on determining guilt? If you personally stand up for your mistakes and failings, if you assume responsibility for your behavior, those around you will notice and will, without thinking, begin to assume responsibility for their actions the same as you. Taking responsibility is the best of all modeling actions we can take. It shows our humility, fosters hope, and reduces our tendency to apply force to achieve our intentions.

When you start singing the "I don't get it when they don't get it" song, just remember it all starts with you. None of us has the power to change another; we can only change ourselves. Focus on what you can do to take responsibility for your behaviors and reactions. What you choose to do and how you do it is the greatest influence you can have in shifting the response of another.

Get It!
Key Two
Force Begets Resistance; Practice Humility

REMEMBER JULIE AND THE Chinese handcuffs? The harder she pulled, the more force was exerted on her fingers, keeping them held firmly and unmovingly in place. It was only when she began to relax that she was able to move them even the slightest bit. And when she ceased resisting, she was able to move freely. Force always begets resistance. If we try to ram behavioral changes down their throats, we can expect firmly clenched teeth, closed lips, and heads turned 180° from where we'd like them to be focused. The more certain we are right, the more likely we are to attempt to enforce our will. Being humble in our knowledge and presentation of that knowledge will reduce the feelings of forced acceptance in the recipients. When they are not feeling pressure, they will not resist; when they do, they will.

Practicing humility requires us to accept that we don't know it all. To be humble is to leave space for the ideas of others, to allow questions to be asked, and to ask for help.

To apply this key, you must be observant. Your clue to change your approach is when others resist your ideas or actions.

Get It!
Key Three
Telling Turns Them Off;
Begin with Questions

NO ONE LIKES TO BE TOLD WHAT to do. It goes against our grain. Interestingly, the less we know the more we defend our limited level of knowledge and the more we resist being told anything new. Most of us are programmed to defend the status quo. If we are asked questions that require our opinion, our input, or our ideas, we are most willing to provide them. The magic comes during this process: Once we have been acknowledged for our expertise, the door has been opened for us to accept the expertise of others. Sharing our wisdom puts us on an equal footing and allows us to accept, without feelings of inferiority, the wisdom of others. Asking questions, however, requires the use of our most important skill: listening, really listening to both the words and the meaning of what's being said to us. The more we ask, the more we learn; the more we learn, the better we teach. And wasn't that the goal in the first place? Showing them how to get it?

Practicing this key involves framing open-ended questions. Attempt to start most conversations with a question and suspend your own thoughts and statements until you have heard the full opinion of the other person. By seeking first to understand, you might find that there is more common ground than difference.

Understanding is the bridge to building a trusting relationship that can support even divergent opinions. Be careful not to label another opinion as wrong or bad. The process of inquiry has the potential to create new and better ways of doing things.

Get It!
Key Four
Being Right Might Be Wrong;
Remain Open

OUR DEFAULT EVALUATION MECHANISM tells us that if you are right, I must be wrong. It is difficult for us to believe that more than one person can be right about the same thing at the same time. While that scenario may actually be more real than not, our initial response only allows one person to be right at a time. Much of this comes from our early years of parent-child interactions where parental controls are biologically in place to keep our offspring safe and well. As we mature, however, our relationships should move past parent-child to adult-adult; often, they do not. Thus, your being right in the face of their not getting it may often be taken by them as a putdown, as a statement that they are wrong. The degree to which you can take right and wrong out of the equation is the degree to which helping them get it will be easier. Avoid being self-righteous in your rightness. Allowing for being wrong will go a long way toward helping them be right.

Chances are that there is more than one way to do anything. If you think you are right, you don't necessarily need to make them feel wrong. To do this, learn to find the merit in everyone's ideas. Give each person the consideration of listening to them fully. Let individuals use the frame of reference they need to understand the concept. Allow them to explain the concept back to you using their terms, not yours.

Get It!
Key Five
If You Believe They Can't,
They Won't;
Believe They Can

WHAT YOU THINK ABOUT THEIR ability to succeed has a great bearing on what they will actually do. Henry Ford said, "Whether you think you can do a thing or cannot do a thing, you are right." If you do not believe they have a chance in the world to succeed, how can they? Why should they? Why would they even try if all-knowing-you do not believe they are able to succeed? Conversely, believe that they can, and let them know constantly that you so believe, and success will arrive sooner than anyone might have thought possible.

If you believe that most people, given consideration and time, will open themselves to learn, grow, and adapt, they will. The attitude you adopt as a teacher/partner will greatly influence whether others take the risk to try to stretch. Practice this key by visualizing a positive interaction and outcome. Communicate with encouraging words and gestures, and strive to authentically demonstrate your belief that together we can surmount any challenge. Optimism is a powerful force that generates the energy needed for transformative experiences. Exercise ways to fuel your source of optimism.

The Get It! Keys
Application

"I DON'T GET IT WHEN THEY DON'T GET IT" isn't necessarily a bad response. It's what we do with that reaction, how we voice it, and what it does to us that is either good, bad, or indifferent. When those around us just don't get it, it's not the end of the world as we know it. It's an opportunity to become a teacher and a partner to see that we all get it together.

Turning resistance into understanding is about advancing our current behaviors along the Get It! Continuum. Our working relationships, our expectations, and how we approach work are always changing and evolving. For us to be successful as individuals, we too must evolve and mature. To improve communications and to support efforts for positive organizational change, our inner actions need to shift. To be effective (within our organizations and personally) we need to be self-evaluative. For example: Do you know how others perceive you? Or how you *want* to be perceived by others? Is how you are *being* creating the results you desire? What would be the benefit to you and others if you were to adopt some new behaviors?

Adopting a new behavior does not necessarily mean throwing out an existing behavior and replacing it with a new one, but rather advancing from an ineffective behavioral position on the Get It! Continuum to one that is more effective, one that will help ensure your continued effectiveness in a world that's changing around you.

Sometimes we get stuck on the continuum; for many reasons, we maintain the same attitudes and behaviors

THE GET IT! CONTINUUM

TAKING RESPONSIBILITY

Blame ◄─────────────► Ownership

When you make the shift toward ownership, you recognize that things might be at least partly your fault, and you accept responsibility.

PRACTICING HUMILITY

Righteous ◄─────────────► Engaging

When you make the shift toward engaging, you realize that your previous efforts have been producing results that were the opposite of your intentions. At this point, you need to ask for help and then accept it unconditionally when it's offered.

BEGINNING WITH QUESTIONS

Telling ◄─────────────► Asking

When you make the shift toward asking, you consciously begin interactions with open-ended questions. These questions are blameless, earnest requests for information that will begin the process of improving communications.

REMAINING OPEN

Judging/Criticizing ◄─────────────► Supporting

When you make the shift toward supporting, you no longer attach or assume negative intentions. You suspend judgment and listen without bias.

BELIEVING THEY CAN

Hedging ◄─────────────► Committing

When you make the shift toward committing, you abandon doubt and negative language and replace them with the power of positive expectation.

for long periods of time. While we are stuck in those positions, the world around is not; it changes and evolves as we spin our wheels. The solution for each of us to get unstuck is to shift our behaviors and advance along the continuum, to continue our life journey of growth.

An effective way to get unstuck is to use Get It! Key Three: Begin with Questions. On the following two pages are eleven questions for reflection and dialogue that you can use by yourself or with others to help you break free and Get It!

Questions for Reflection and Dialogue

1 • When Julie said, "I don't get it when they don't get it," what scenarios in your own life did that make you think of?

2 • What do you do when you find yourself saying "I don't get it when they don't get it"?
  • What is your first impulse?
  • What alternate impulse/response did the parable cause you to consider?

3 • What result might you get if you asked yourself, "What could I do or say that would help them understand what they need to know to succeed?" and then applied your answer?

4 • What kind of environment supports others in finding the information they need to realize their own change?
  • Do you foster that environment?
  • If not, what changes do you need to make to create one?

5 • How can you model behaviors that will illustrate the desired state? How can you create opportunities for them to try on new styles or behaviors without becoming endangered?

6 • What behaviors/thoughts/actions did Julie use to prevent herself from getting it?
- What is in the way of their getting it?
- Of your getting it?
- How do you challenge that comfort zone respectfully?

7 • What questions can you ask others to promote open exploration of their hopes, fears, and aspirations?

8 • Madame Nosall told Julie that everybody acted superior when someone to whom they were trying to explain something didn't get it. Do you recall a situation where you felt someone was thinking you were stupid?
- How did you feel about that?
- Have you ever been guilty of thinking that way about others?

9 • What successes have *you* had in transforming people?
- Which were you able to transform: their beliefs, their behaviors, or their opinions?
- Describe your keys to fostering understanding.

10 • What improvement in the result, and the process leading to that result, have you noticed occurring when transformation does take place in you, them, or both?
- In what ways is it worth the effort?

11 • Describe or discuss a situation in which you could apply each of the five keys.

About the Authors

LESLIE YERKES

One thing you can say about Leslie Yerkes is that she gets it. Another thing you can say is that she knows how  to make sure that *you* get it. In her job as an organizational development/ change management consultant, Leslie has helped thousands to get it and to learn how to make sure that those around them get it, too.

A graduate of Wittenberg University and Case Western Reserve University, Leslie is the founder of Catalyst Consulting Group, Inc. in Cleveland, Ohio. She has taught at John Carroll University, Baldwin Wallace College, and is on the faculty at the Weatherhead Dively Center for Executive Education.

Leslie's business goal is to help people create sustainable organizations. Her life goal is to create a framework in which people can draw on their own resources to find creative solutions. Her clients have included Chrysler Corporation, The Cleveland Clinic Foundation, Lake Hospital System, The United Church of America, Westfield Companies, and ISG: International Steel Group. A sub-specialty of Leslie's is making non-profits healthy and sustainable.

Yerkes is the author of three previous books that have been translated into more than a dozen languages and sold hundreds of thousands of copies worldwide.

RANDY MARTIN

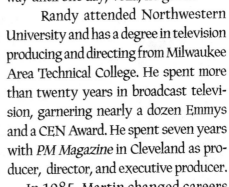

For six months, Randy didn't get the concept of this book. But Leslie continued in a gentle, non-threatening way until one day, voilá, he got it!

Randy attended Northwestern University and has a degree in television producing and directing from Milwaukee Area Technical College. He spent more than twenty years in broadcast television, garnering nearly a dozen Emmys and a CEN Award. He spent seven years with *PM Magazine* in Cleveland as producer, director, and executive producer.

In 1985, Martin changed careers and started the award-winning martinDESIGN, a marketing/advertising firm that "Reframes people's thoughts and makes them powerful, profitable, and enlightening." His clients have included: Stop-n-Shop Supermarkets, Tony Roma's, Focus Four, The Cleveland Growth Association, The Cleveland Ballet, Reflections Interior Design, and Catalyst Consulting Group.

In addition to writing and designing, Martin teaches business courses for ResultsPlus and Focus Four, writes an Internet column on NeanderthalsForAmerica.com, is the executive director of Rock and Roll Fantasy Weekend in Memphis, and plays lost classics on the guitar. He is a high school girls soccer coach and is working on an instructional soccer book called *First Man and The Short Game: How to Create Great Teams Using Average Players.*

About the Illustrator

BEN DEWEY

Ben Dewey is a freelance illustrator and graduate of The Cleveland Institute of Art (CIA). He is the recipient of CIA's Mary C. Page Traveling Scholarship (for the top painting student of the year) and the Sue Wall Painting Scholarship. His Bachelor of Fine Arts project on legendary blues guitarist Roscoe Porter earned him a spot in the Top Twenty Final Presentation, a prestigious evaluation and award.

Dewey has been drawing since childhood and playing electric and slide guitar since the age of thirteen. He has created band performance posters for the tours of several national recording artists and currently plays guitar with several groups in the Cleveland area while pursing a career in the comics industry.

He is the author of the soon-to-be-released single, "Moonshine Boys."

Contacts

Leslie Yerkes
Catalyst Consulting Group, Inc.
12701 Larchmere Blvd, Suite 4A
Cleveland OH 44120
216-791-7802
fax: 216-791-7860

fun@catalystconsulting.net
www.changeisfun.com

Randy Martin
martinDESIGN
2140 Lee Road
Suite 209
Cleveland OH 44118
216-397-7975

martinDESIGN@ameritech.net

Ben Dewey
lapstyle@yahoo.com

Resources

The following support materials are currently available to assist you in creating an organizational culture that will help all members to get it!

KEYNOTE SPEECHES AND WORKSHOPS

Energize your organization or your next meeting or conference with a fun presentation that sparks everyone's desire to understand and be understood, to get it!

VIDEO PROGRAM

Based on the book *They Just Don't Get It!*, this video is in production and will be available soon.

TRAINING MATERIALS

A variety of assessment tools and programs are available that can be customized to your organization to assist you and your staff/ownership in fostering understanding throughout. Tools range from simple questionnaires to day-long programs, to the complete Get It! campaign.

For information on these and other resources, please contact us at:

Catalyst Consulting Group, Inc.
12701 Larchmere Blvd, Suite 4A
Cleveland, OH 44120
Phone: 216-791-7802
Fax: 216-791-7860
fun@catalystconsulting.net
www.changeisfun.com
www.Get-It-Campaign.com

Notes

Notes

Notes

Notes

Notes

Notes

Notes

Berrett-Koehler Publishers

Berrett-Koehler is an independent publisher of books and other publications at the leading edge of new thinking and innovative practice on work, business, management, leadership, stewardship, career development, human resources, entrepreneurship, and global sustainability.

Since the company's founding in 1992, we have been committed to creating a world that works for all by publishing books that help us to integrate our values with our work and work lives, and to create more humane and effective organizations.

We have chosen to focus on the areas of work, business, and organizations, because these are central elements in many people's lives today. Furthermore, the work world is going through tumultuous changes, from the decline of job security to the rise of new structures for organizing people and work. We believe that change is needed at all levels—individual, organizational, community, and global—and our publications address each of these levels.

To find out about our new books,
special offers,
free excerpts,
and much more,
subscribe to our free monthly eNewsletter at

www.bkconnection.com

Please see next pages for other books
from Berrett-Koehler Publishers

Fun Works
Creating Places
Where People Love to Work

Leslie Yerkes

Leslie Yerkes provides proven tools to unleash the power of fun and make the workplace a winning experience for workers, clients, customers, vendors, and stakeholders alike. It provides a comprehensive set of guiding principles any organization can apply to increase satisfaction and meaning at work by accessing the life-giving force of fun.

Paperback • ISBN 1-57675-154-6 • Item #51546-415 $17.95

301 Ways to Have Fun at Work
Dave Hemsath and Leslie Yerkes
Illustrated by Dan McQuillen

In this entertaining and comprehensive guide, Hemsath and Yerkes show readers how to have fun at work—everyday. Written for anyone who works in any type of organization, *301 Ways to Have Fun at Work* provides more than 300 ideas for creating a dynamic, fun-filled work environment.

Paperback • ISBN 1-57675-019-1 • Item #50191-415 $16.95

You Don't Have to Do It Alone
How to Involve Others
to Get Things Done

Richard H. Axelrod, Emily M. Axelrod,
Julie Beedon, and Robert W. Jacobs

You need to involve others in order to achive your goals, and this book shows how to take a systematic approach. Organized around a series of five questions, the book offers helpful tools and techniques for resolving them, as well as providing examples from corporations, government, and the nonprofit sector.

Paperback • ISBN 1-57675-278-X • Item #5278X-415 $16.95

Berrett-Koehler Publishers
PO Box 565, Williston, VT 05495-9900
Call toll-free! **800-929-2929** 7 am-9 pm EST
Or fax your order to 1-802-864-7626
For fastest service order online: **www.bkconnection.com**

PeopleSmart
Developing Your
Interpersonal Intelligence

Mel Silberman, Ph.D., with
Freda Hansberg, Ph.D.

Details the eight essential skills of interpersonal intelligence and provides a powerful plan for becoming more effective in every relationship—with supervisors, coworkers, a spouse, family, and friends.

Paperback • ISBN 1-57675-091-4 • Item #50914-415 $18.95

Working PeopleSmart
6 Strategies for Success

Mel Silberman, Ph.D. and
Freda Hansburg, Ph.D.

Describes the six core strategies used by people-smart individuals and shows how to apply them in the toughest workplace situations.

Paperback • ISBN 1-57675-208-9 • Item #52089-415 $18.95

Developing Your PeopleSmart Skills
A Handbook Series

This booklet series makes the invaluable lessons of the book *PeopleSmart* available in an inexpensive and easily distributed format.

Asserting Your Needs ISBN 1-58376-160-8, Item #61608-415

Being a Team Player ISBN 1-58376-164-0, Item #61640-415

Changing Tactics ISBN 1-58376-165-9, Item #61659-415

Exchanging Feedback ISBN 1-58376-161-6, Item #61616-415

Expressing Yourself Clearly ISBN 1-58376-159-4
Item #61594-415

Influencing Others ISBN 1-58376-162-4, Item #61624-415

Resolving Conflict ISBN 1-58376-163-2, Item #61632-415

Understanding People ISBN 1-58376-158-6, Item #61586-415

Each booklet: paperback, 32-48 pages, $7.95

Berrett-Koehler Publishers
PO Box 565, Williston, VT 05495-9900
Call toll-free! **800-929-2929** 7 am-9 pm EST

Or fax your order to 1-802-864-7626
For fastest service order online: **www.bkconnection.com**